ERODING WITNESS

ERODING WITNESS

POEMS BY NATHANIEL MACKEY

University of Illinois Press

Urbana and Chicago

The National Poetry Series was established in 1978 to publish five collections of poetry annually through five participating publishers. The manuscripts are selected by five poets of national reputation. Publication is funded by James A. Michener, Edward J. Piszek, the Copernicus Society of America, the Ford Foundation, the Mobil Foundation, Exxon Corporation, the Polaroid Foundation, and the five publishers—E. P. Dutton, University of Georgia Press, Graywolf Press, University of Illinois Press, and Persea Press.

The National Poetry Series, 1984

Amy Bartlett, *Afterwards* (Selected by Galway Kinnell), Persea Press
Kathy Fagan, *The Raft* (Selected by Daniel Halpern), E. P. Dutton
Robert L. Jones, *Wild Onion* (Selected by Carolyn Forché), Graywolf Press
Nathaniel Mackey, *Eroding Witness* (Selected by Michael Harper),
    University of Illinois Press
Bruce Smith, *Silver & Information* (Selected by Hayden Carruth),
    University of Georgia Press

This book is printed on acid-free paper.

Acknowledgments: Thanks to the editors of the following periodicals in which some of these poems appeared.
Alcatraz: "Ghede Poem"
Boxcar: "Song of the Andoumboulou: 3," "Winged Abyss," "The Phantom Light of All Our Day"
Calafia: "Poem for Don Cherry"
Credences: "Song of the Andoumboulou: 5," "Song of the Andoumboulou: 7," "Ohnedaruth's Day Begun"
Gumbo: "The Shower of Secret Things"
Hambone: "Song of the Andoumboulou: 1," "Song of the Andoumboulou: 2," "Song of the Andoumboulou: 4"
The Iowa Review: "Black Snake Visitation," "Tarot-Teller," "Grisgris Dancer"
Isthmus: "Waters . . . ," "Kiche Manitou," "Dream Thief," "The Shower of Secret Things: 3," *"and when the Moon struck," "enuma elish 2,"* " 'Her boat of sun's burnt . . . ,' " "The Canals"
New World Journal: "Passing Thru"
Quarry West: "Outer Egypt," "Capricorn Rising," "Memphite Recension"
River Styx: "Parlay Cheval Ou," "Song of the Andoumboulou: 6," " 'John Coltrane Arrived with An Egyptian Lady' "
Yardbird Reader: "New and Old Gospel"

Library of Congress Cataloging in Publication Data

Mackey, Nathaniel, 1947–
    Eroding witness.

    (National poetry series)
    I. Title.   II. Series.
PS3563.A3166E7   1985   811'.54   85–1010
ISBN 0-252-01230-5   (alk. paper)

For Gloria,

and to

the memory of my grandmother,

Nancy Fuller Wilcox

Contents

IV Septet for the End of Time

These poems are about prophecy and initiation; the uncompromising narratives that sing but *don't explain* are the sounds of a mythmaker-griot in the midst of ceremonial talk, the totems of incantation, the way to the source, the origins of power. That so much of the authentication, roadmaps of Anthropology, are dreams of return, the result of the diaspora—that they honor musicians, Coltrane, Jimi Hendrix—that they restore connectives to Ananse the spider, to devotions, to shamanism, is the reconstruction of a spiritual wholeness despite the fragmentation of the body. To give testimony to the sources of light, however eroding as missives of song, is continuous visitation, promises of psychic restitution for what has been undone, and done over, well.

Michael S. Harper

Waters
wet the
mouth. Salt
currents come
to where the
lips, thru
which the tongue
slips, part.

At the tongue's
tip the sting
of saltish
metal rocks
the wound. A
darkness there
    like tar,
like bits of
drift at ocean's
edge. A slow

retreat of
waters beaten
back upon
themselves.

    An undertow
of whir im-
mersed in
        words.

Parlay Cheval Ou

Heard
horsehairs
 coiled in rain-
water hiss,
 watched
rainwater turn
 to stone

Stood lame,
 limped,
undulant earth
 our twisted
feet, first
 odors of
want, bambooish
 odors of
bone. . .

Forever
felt for
 the hem of
her skirt
 as though
falling,
 with a glimpse
of her hips
 would go
down. . .

Ghost of
crossings,
 begged Erzulie
be kind, un-
 cloud our

knowing, wet
   Ouranos
worm our
  roots up
out the
   ground

Kiche Manitou

The ground
itself would
hint at

what this was
whose name
I'd read,

each tree a
rumor, all
but gone

from where
I'd lived,
no air

got in.
However good
to get the

sweat out
felt I
stumbled,

even fell,
and where that
plunge was

where what
world there
was, did

word rise
up from

where tongues

reach to,
our mouths
all muddy

from the
dive. Then
were tortoises,

boars, later
loons as
word spread

eastward, out-
ward out of
Asia cross

the straits
whose wet
earth wormed.

Twisted,
catch of
mud where

blood the
moon drinks
up, unborn,

till even
wisdoms rub
clean

of regret
or go wanting,
where doubt,

to where
all but
disaster,

walks.

      •

I awoke
ahead of
myself, got

out of the
tent, went
out for wood,

some of it
wet but
lit, the

flame sucked
up by wind,
some dead

thing's
whisper.
Stuttered,

in my throat
what risk
of talk

no wind
would take,
the lure,

the tug of
bones recess
from touch

announces,
talks as
if there was

in that
which blows
against

the first
a second
wind, yet in

whose way
the older
fires which

are ferns
reverse
themselves,

and spores
go up and
out from

what before
were un-
dersides.

Dream Thief

That what
they think
undoes
the lures

does nothing
at all
doesn't
even occur

(or ever
does) to
them but once,
if once

it had
they'd watch
her bathe
and when

she rose
not ring the
tub with
what they'd

see. A
door. Once
thru this
door they'd

sit in-
structed,
(songs) take
hold of

"her," all
twisted mat
of hair
but ooze

of salt from
where she's
cut, that
there'd be

nowhere else
to go but
where she'd
gone, where

gulls, the
sea goes,
on. They'd
go, not

being bothered
by that
none of it
would last,

that only
then they'd
have their
skins cut,

answer come
to what
she'd ask:
What is

the white
water
restless by
night?

•

Except an old
man speak
of tongues,
these

having been
hid, housing
all he'd
say, though

all he'd say
was that
"they" would,
not where.

But that the
spot grew
warm where
these tongues

were put
in he'd put
in boxes
hid so all

not having
seen not
have to, blind

but having

heard: Her
cloth undone,
she'd black
their eyes

out, sun show
signs of
her none but
he'd see.

The Shower of Secret Things

1

They ask her
what she'd think
if what she
thought was rock

shook and
rumbled like
hunger, if
what moved inside

the rock was
not its
blood but an
itch on their

tongues. And
where the bones,
what it was
they'd be, refused

its care love
quit its rattle,
while what
blood was in

the rock went
to their
heads (heads wet
with voices),

each its own,
each as it

was (the way they
were), beside

themselves.

2

There was a
man it seems,
whispered himself
thru his

fingers, a
cloth between
her legs, the fabric
wet from her

insides, her
ragged crotch, who
when she'd rise
would look him

down, or so
she'd say. And
this man, she says,
walks thru

her house, has
no clothes
on and carries
himself like her

Twin. Walks her
where when it

rains it not only
pours but

appears to be
sun. And burns like
salt the sand
does, and there

does a dance until
the sun cracks
her lips, the
cracks bleed. The

blood cooks,
drought lures
the "witch"
toward where the

bank they stand
on is. They
throw her in,
and that the river

wet her hair
predicted rain.

Grisgris Dancer

Backwardswalking
twoheaded
woman. Bony

feet down to
which I
bow but will not

be spared.
Stored pressings of
earth in its

red way sourced
in its own
embrace, all

the grudges of time.
All the gathered
ache of our

severed selves,
all the
windowless light.

And of the Beyond,
that the
witnesses lie

gratefully goes
without telling. That
the aberrant

earth, overrun
by birds and

unshod of all

image, greets a
manyfisted
sun. That the

backwardswalking
woman, taken
up thru the air by

the scruff of
her neck by
hoisted snakeskin

towropes, hurries back
down to be
one with us,

beginnings again
gone up
in smoke.

Black Snake Visitation

for Jimi Hendrix

A black tantric
snake I dream
two days to the

morning I die
slipping up
thru my throat,

slithers out
like the vomit I'll
be choked by

can't, gigantic
seven-headed
snake, sticks out

one head at a
time. Must
be this hiss my

guitar's been
rehearsing
sits me down by

where the salt
water crosses the
sweet. Self-

searching twitch,
the scrawny
light of its

carriage, broken
sealit stark-
ness, furtive

sea of regrets.
But not re-
duced by what

I knew would not
matter, woke
to see no one

caress the arisen
wonder's dreamt-of
thigh. Death

enters a slack
circle whispering,
slapping hands,

beauty baited
like a hook, hurt
muse at whose

feet whatever
fruit I'd give goes
abruptly bad.

*Must be this
hiss my
guitar's*

*been rehearsing,
lizardquick
tongues like*

*they were
licking the sky.*

Must be this
hiss my
guitar's been

rehearsing, these
lizardquick tongues
like they

were licking
the sky.

Down on my
knees testing
notes with

my teeth, always
knew a day'd
come I'd

put my wings out
and fly.

Ghede Poem

They call me Ghede. The butts
of "angels" brush my lips.

The soiled asses of "angels"
    touch my lips, I
kiss the gap of their having
        gone. They call me Ghede, I
    sit, my chair tilted, shin across
thigh.

They call me Ghede
of the Many-Colored Cap, the
Rising Sun. I suck
                breath from this
inner room's midearth's bad air,
                make chair
    turn into chariot,
                    swing.

They call me
Ghede-Who-Even-Eats-His-Own-Flesh,
                        the Rising

    Sun. I say, "You love, I love, he
        love, she love. What does
all this loving make?"

They call me Ghede of
the Nasal Voice, they leave
    me for dead outside
        the eighteenth wall.
                    The seven
    winds they leave in charge
                    of me sing,
say like I say they say, say,

"You love, I
love, he love, she love. What
does all this loving
                              make?

                    What
does all this loving make exactly
here on this the edge of love's
                              disappearance,
the naked weight of all sourceness
thrust like thieves thru inexhaustible
                    earth, ashen odors of
buttsweat, hell's breath,
                              what
does all this loving
                              make?"

On this the edge of love's disappearance
          the sun and moon of no worship
          lodge their light between your palms.
          They call me Ghede but
                              they
                                        reverse themselves,
the sweaty press of all flesh, my fever's
                              growth, soaps,
                    alms.

And on this the edge of love's
                              disappearance
          painted wafers of bread go quietly
          stale beneath your tongue.
                              Your
          throated moans attempt a line
you call He-Most-High, some intangible

thrust, one whose bodiless touch
                                        you try to
approximate as "Light."

                    Yes, they call me
            Ghede of the Many-Colored Cap, the
            Rising Sun. I make the hanged
                                        man
            supply his own rope, I gargle rum,
                    the points of knives grow more
            and more sharp underneath your skin.

                                        My name is
            Ghede-Who-Gets-Under-Your-Skin, my medicinal dick
                    so erect it shines, the slow
                    cresting of stars astride a bed
                        of unrest gives my foreskin the
                        sheen of a raven's wings,
                                        the
            untranslatable shouts of a previous church my
                school of ointments, my attendants
            keep a logbook of signs.

                    They call me
Ghede-Who-Beside-The-River-Sits-With-His-Knees-
            Pulled-Up-To-His-Chest, the warm
                                        swill of
                thrown rum sloshing down between my
                                        feet
                while in my horse's face whole boatloads
            of assfat explode.

                        Ghede of the Technicolored Kiss

24

I'm sometimes called and sometimes
Ghede-No-Knotted-Cloth-Gets-In-Whose-Way.
"You love, I love, he love, she
love. What does all this loving make?"
is what I say between two lips whose
                              ill-starred
          openings give out light.

                         "What
does all this loving make exactly here
                              on this
          the edge of love's disappearance, the
          naked weight of all sourceness thrust
                                   like thieves
     thru inexhaustible earth, ashen odors of
          buttsweat, hell's breath, what
                                   does all this
               loving make?"

                    On this the edge
     of love's disappearance you sit enthroned before
          an unsuspected dinner of thorns.
                              As you go down you
wake to see yourself marooned off the coast of
          Georgia, captive singers in the Moving
Star Hall still averse to what hurts your
          heart swells to encompass, a
                         soot-faced
          boatman in the Peacock's house,
                              hands
heavy with mud.
                    Hands heavy with the mist of your
               own belated breath, as you come up
                    you feel your mouth fill with graveyard

dirt, the skinny fingers of dawn
thump a funky piano, the
tune three parts honky-tonk, two parts church.

Yes, they call me Ghede of the Many-Colored Cap,
the Rising Sun. I make the hanged man
supply his own rope, I gargle rum, the
points of knives grow more and more
sharp underneath your
skin.

My name is Ghede-Who-Gets-Under-Your-Skin,
Ghede-Whose-Heart-Sits-Elsewhere-Shrouded-In-Dew.
"You love, I love, he love, she love . . . "

Ghede.
The name is Ghede.
The tossed asses of
"angels"
anoint my lips.

The Shower of Secret Things: 3

—how the shame got put in shaman—

That where the earth shook what inside
was not its bones, but what
burned it,
            blood.
      In a truck
somewhere south of DaNang they
hit a mine,
            and that the
truck was blown apart
   and by what was
a flash they were thrown from it,
      all but him killed. . .

      This is what the
newsmen said:
            "All except fire burns.
                        But the woman in the woods
      was of a longing you mistook,
         looked at, taken up
                  into but lost,

                  her tattered look
                              was only one of what
                  were phases read
                              from some engraver's book."

      "Which phrase?"
                  was my second mistake.

      And where the street
   shook, what inside
was neither blood nor what
                  stayed it, stone.
            "Bone. My flute struck bone,"

said the shaman.
        "The noise cut
inside me like
        a knife inside a clam."
                        Drunk, and he'd just driven
                his car up my back, then
                said that, no, it
                        wasn't his, "*you* clean it up."

                        Then when the darkness
                broke I'd slept and some
                        wheel slipped and run
                                        thru me up thru my
                        skin where she'd
walked.

                Head all plump with
                        women, put the night's eye out and thought,
                saw,
                        called it a voice
                I'd heard say no,

                        that they had all gone.
                Or would go, and that
        she, only she'd be there
                        then, all these others entered
into after her, there where the

                                elm stood, clues,
                        the others clues
                                to where she's kept . . .

                Then again outside, the
                        same dark, the same road you don't

see. The same
trucks, that when they've gone

you don't even notice.

II
Song of the Andoumboulou

The song of the Andoumboulou is addressed to the spirits. For this reason the initiates, crouching in a circle, sing it in a whisper in the deserted village, and only the howling of dogs and the wind disturb the silence of the night.

—François Di Dio, liner notes to *Les Dogon* (Disques Ocora)

"You speak of 'making' people 'believe.' Was there then something secret, which they were not to know?"

"If you wanted to explain what happened to someone who knew nothing about it, to an ordinary man, you would say that a power came down from heaven to eat the old man and change his bones into beneficent stones."

"But what is the truth?"

"If one wanted to explain it to you, a Nazarene, one would say that someone came down from heaven like a woman with a woman's dress and ornaments, and ate the old man, and that the stones are not his bones but her ornaments."

— Marcel Griaule, *Conversations with Ogotemmêli*

Song of the Andoumboulou: 1

The song says the
dead will not
ascend without song.

That because if
we lure them their names get
our throats, the
word sticks.

As not
more than a week
before when she
did, that it read they'd return,
turn out one day

our mouths
touch, *Tutor*

me, teach me this
thirst.

Then in the eighth book
warned of a Sea,
        that it brings them in, that

    born of waves,
a wash of
            words inside

        our throats,
    its bottomless voice's
            brew of stems turns our insides out. . .

            Or like these new ones they'd
    explain,
            these Others,
"fish that walk on land,"
                    the signs
        are old men drunk on

                        sidewalks,
                    mumblers. . .

                The dead, they say, *are dying*
        of thirst,

    not even words.
        Except it says itself
    for days

        in your head.

                    •

And that voice, the
book says, drinks blood
but will tell you
        the dead don't want
us bled, but to be
        sung.

        And she said the same,
    a thin wisp of soul,
But I want the meat of
    my body sounded.

            Drummed,
    I put in, played
upon by hands,
            hers,
        made a "priest" of . . .

            Faces, run
        out by water.
            Features waste and reappear.

    Boathouses
        haunt the fog,
horns gossip.

        Heads nod, maracas.
    Emptied out of
        all but seeds.

Song of the Andoumboulou: 2

The nubbed white remains of her hands.

        Surrounds herself
               with easy men. A moist
     hole matted with hair.

           And who
         are they, whose
         attentions she
     prolongs but won't
            remember?
      Always scrubbed,
          rehearsed, regretted,

forgiven like a whore forgives
   her body.

        And at always
     the same hour,
        the same
      angle, the
          same thickness,

the same shadow crosses
   the ground.

         An arm goes
forward. Each finger finds
      its limit.

         The distance

persists, like a grudge.

•

And as you come to where she does,

        to where the sky
    walks houses cave
        in, even caves
        collapse.

              Her hands
   get back their fingers,
            wind in your teeth
        as you grin, you
   want kisses,

           tell lies.
Lies, then twists her
        lips, whose frown you
         test,

            her chapped mouth.

   Cool thumbs lubricate the
hinge of her thigh.
        On down the
    street she

         does a
       dance,
        turns,

  throws her ass, the ocean

      in it.

•

An enclosure. Each wave is as to grasp

                    is an enclosure.
                              Others of it
                    fade, let go as
                         waste the
                                   tides pull up, the
          moon takes.

Wet sand and water
              wet our feet, all
          shore dissolves,

                         as at our
                    bed's edge each
                              finger

                    works the ribs of

                    broken ships.

Song of the Andoumboulou: 3

            Mute Serqet. Inside
            her head
                no house
            inside itself,
                        no sun.

                What song there
            was delivered up to
                above where sound leaves off,

        though whatever place words talk us
                        into'd be like hers,
                    who'd only speak
            to herself . . .

(A hill, down thru
            its hole only ants
        where this
                was. The mud

                    hut was her body.)

            Embraced, but
    on the edge of speech
            though she spoke

            without words,
                    as in a dream.

                    The loincloth, he
            said, is tight,
                    which is so that it conceals
                    the woman's sacred parts.
        But that in him

this worked a longing
        to unveil what's underneath,

    the Word the Nommo
            put inside the fabric's
        woven secret,

                the Book wherein
    the wet of kisses
                keeps.

                •

            Mouth that moved my mouth
        to song, her
            mouth would not be
                touched.

        She kept to one side of
my talk
    like a man, to

                herself.

            My lips moved, a
                music.
                    Unheard of.

40

While chromolithographs and plaster images of the Catholic saints are prominently displayed in the shrines and houses of the santeros, they are regarded only as empty ornaments or decorations, which may be dispensed with. The real power of the santos resides in the stones, hidden behind a curtain in the lower part of the altar, without which no santería shrine could exist. The most powerful stones are said to have been brought from Africa by the slaves, who concealed them in their stomachs by swallowing them.

— William R. Bascom, "The Focus of Cuban Santería"

Song of the Andoumboulou: 4

What they'll say was a
calling marks the
            whites of his
  thighs with
            gifts of charred

            bread.
The milkish
            meat of corn,
  the god's ear
      sweet but infected
            with hair. The
god's hand dips our
            sleeves in
      vinegar, blown
            rain's whispers
repeat themselves.

            The dead, they say, *are*
            dying of

thirst, not even
words,

except it says itself
for days
in your head.

•

The light arrives wrapped in

shadows,   which
in the blown
sweat of gold
between the legs

of kept
women   help
the wind in
thru the
cracks between   our teeth.

The light arrives wrapped
in bread, in   broken
voices,
the napes
of our   necks bibbed in

rust as we   awaken.
The light arrives   wrapped
in dust.

The light

arrives

                        wrapped in
        spoons full of
                kisses,
                                skillets
        full of raindrops,
                        made of wood.
The light
                arrives wrapped

                in drums,   in drawn

                        curtains.   The rocks

        inside our stomachs

                        want blood.

Song of the Andoumboulou: 5

—gassire's lute—

And because I was lost

because I labored in the throes
        of an angry birth,

she bides her time, become
        as one with her bed
of light.
            "Sad bringer of love,
            born singer of sorrow,"
                                she warns
        me, "beware the false beauty
of loss,
            I warn you beware the
            burnt odor of blood you
                say we ask of you,

    bewail the sad limits of
                choice . . .
                        Remember this:
        that all ascent moves up
        a stairway of shattered
                                light . . .

The least eye's observance of
        dawn will endanger what
                                of love

    you take as one with 'love's bite.' "

                •

In the village of the dead this is how it is:

Sweatborn you eat the smell of
dog's hair, painted food.
                    Nuns in suede habits walk by.

                    Manzanita's tinge among
the leaves, eyes old as timber.
    Musk old bone's dead whiskers "catch."

                    So then the day begins to
    breathe again. Scorched clouds
        red around its edges,

                                        purple sun.
            Curtains, quilt of
        turtleshell,
                        she parts.

Adept, she emerges hand
            over hand, absorbs what
        little sun there is

        left.   Fallen asleep, four
    times, to rise later,
            wake to rout what
                            lay between
us,
        melt our teeth.

                ·

            Dried seeds
    brush the gourds'
        inner skins,
    the escaping song's

      inward reach of sea
some all too endable
                 assent.

Chiselled rock. Rude
  squawk of birds.
(Her buttocks bulge
  with emulsified light.)

        Dawn so belated I wept,
  would've cut its tongues,

    having been denied
Erzulie's inmost
           aye.

        •

        The slight
  rub of untongued
voices.
      The splintered
  reed of our Moroccan moan.

    Dawn, so divisive
      all our taut strings toll
  its exit,
        leaves
our lamps as ever
           yet
        to be lit.

        •

                    But come the
        light of such inward-reaching
            rites we'd strum the
                        rim of

        her starred
        behind's
                hubbed earth,

the lights of some inviolable
                        City,
        thoughts gathered like
            beads, round
        a witch's
                neck.

        All knot of
        thumbs, round
                    each other
    like vines we'd
        vomit light,

            would let
    each breath imbibe an
                inlet

            of dust.

(ii)

*—black
reconstruction—*

and when it
came time to
reach I'd
wavered,
sought you
with hands which,
    hands only
in thought, were
all thumbs.
                All
ears though, how it
seemed, all else
of it hazed away,
once here, how what
was music used it,
    you.

            Then saw the sun
show thru your dress,
and your thighs. And
dark there between
them, and hair, but
what held me:

    Your voice.
That if at
all you spoke,
                it
        sang.

(iii)

                        so we sing,
              as if in the place of
                    some remembered hall,
some recollected joining,

    the instants outdistancing
touch, dead air dusted
        clean of any inmost
                              want

    And where the last
          eye relinquishes
                          floods
    (as when an image lingers,
        lamps, as ever, yet
        to be lit), where one
                          we knew
    whose Name was light now
        writes *There is no song,*
                              except
        its blood crawl up our throats
    each night

    (crawl up our throats
    each
night

Song of the Andoumboulou: 6

Dear Angel of Dust,

In one of your earlier letters, the one you wrote in response to *Song of the Andoumboulou: 3,* you spoke of sorting out "what speaks of speaking of something, and what (more valuably) speaks *from* something, i.e., where the source is available, becomes a re-source rather than something evasive, elusive, sought after." Well, what I wanted to say then was this: We not only can but should speak of "loss" or, to avoid, quotation marks notwithstanding, any such inkling of self-pity, speak of *absence* as unavoidably an inherence in the texture of things (dreamseed, habitual cloth). You really do seem to believe in, to hold out for some first or final gist underlying it all, but my preoccupation with origins and ends is exactly that: a pre- (equally post-, I suppose) occupation.

Tonight my mind struggles, for example, to reject all reminder of thought. It doubles up in some extravagant way as if to ask you back the question always implied by that scowl of yours. But the truth is that I don't even believe any such question exists. I see the things of your world as *solid* in a way the world my "myriad words" uncoil can't even hope to be. *Not* "ethereal," mind you. Not insubstantial, unreal or whatever else. Only an other (possibly Other) sort of solidarity, as if its very underseams—or, to be more exact, those of its advent—sprouted hoofs. (Or as if the Sun, which had come to boat us both away, might've extended horns.) What was wanted least but now comes to be missed *is* that very absence, an unlikely Other whose inconceivable occupancy glimpses of ocean beg access to.

Not "re-source" so much for me as re: Source.

Yours,
N.

cc: Jack Spicer
    García Lorca
    H-mu

The metaphor of the potter is commonly used to describe God's creative activity. Believing that God shapes children in the mother's womb, Banyarwanda women of a child-bearing age are careful to leave water ready, before they go to bed, so that God may use it to create children for them. It is known as "God's water."

—John S. Mbiti, *African Religions and Philosophy*

Song of the Andoumboulou: 7

—ntsikana's bell—

A dark head sits brooding its
image. Where the light
        breaks our need evolves.

    All those other
                        earlier
    entrances of light it
        now wants to recollect
        come crashing to the
floor, so many repeats
                        of an incumbent
        loss.

        And where the space
lights up an old affliction rears
    its head. The tide pulls
                        in again at once
        thru the swell of some lust,
                some exploded
    sun.

                    This, I

heard my own self say,
                    the
new day,
          begins . . .

                    •

Beside our bed a bowl of ready
    water, though we dance
upon the graves of the
        yet-to-be-born.
                        Awaiting
    birth,
            by which or in which a potter-god
could wet what clay would catch
    the flow of our endangered blood.

Here where the feuds root some
    unsunned angel of loss ekes out
        its plunder.
                    Possessed,
    we lick the salt of
        each infected wound's
        unyielding rhythm's wordings.

    "Whipped on, preached at, kicked.
Made a christ
            of.

        Whipped on, preached
    at, kicked. Made a
                    christ of.

    Whipped on, preached at,
        kicked. Made a christ
                    of . . ."

(ii)

By now the angels'
   awaited entrance
   averts our remorse,
       resurrects old wants.

West of us an Eastward
      reach of storm lit up in
patches. Possessed, I
   stroke the baobab's rooty wood,

whose various branchings
   echo this, our
   remembered song.

           "So let
the ladders pierce our
   hearts, Mujadji's
        wrath

renew the earth, a wet
   Sun swirl its milk
   in our throats,

        this body of
     water's dark flesh
       thread floods of new
  light,

    loose clouds
rub each other

      like thighs."

Dear Angel of Dust,

In last night's poem (which I've yet to write) the two of us were singing in some distant "church." A combination acoustic/electric "church" in which the floorboards splintered while something like leg-irons gave our voices their weight. I call it the Heartbreak Church. It sits on an island known as Wet Sun, which itself sits only a mile or so southeast of the Heartbreak Straits. Henry Dumas wrote about it in that story of his, "Ark of Bones."

But what to say about birth? I see the fact of it as so basic and at the same time baseless as to always float free of any such sense of an "about." We've had this quarrel before of course. A Supreme Friction I've decided to call it, even though I've been accused of upwardly displacing sex ("loose clouds/rub each other/like thighs"), of being at base merely obsessed with fucking. Fuck that. I'm just trying to get it into both our heads that to unbend—I often envision you as Nut—that to unbend is to misconceive or miscarry, to want to be done with any relational coherence, to want to abort. You can't continue to want the whole bleeding, flooding fact of it intact without a cut somewhere. "God's water" by itself won't do.

But in that poem last night a dislocated rib quoted you as calling birth a bad pun on "the place where a ship lies at anchor." I applaud your levity. Of late I'd taken to calling you the Bone Goddess because of this irritable wish of yours for what you call rigor. However much I may in the end/beginning turn out to have been courting a lack, I intend to keep that tail-biting lizard in mind. Aren't we all, however absurdly, amputees? Call me Mule-Face all you like. Who the hell cares.

Speaking of birth, get that album *Minas* by Milton Nascimento, the Brazilian singer I told you about. Take special note of the fourth cut on the first side. Don't you hear something "'eartical" or "churchical" (some Rastafarian words I've picked up lately) in it? A certain arch and/or ache and/or ark of duress, the frazzled edge of what remains "unsung"?

Enough for now.

As ever,
N.

and when the Moon struck

soon, all sun put back
inside the ground, the
Way gone,

would all go down
to on all fours,
wear shells and

furs and chase
our tracks

—*enuma elish 2*

        waters the colors of mud, thick
            bush of hairs my bed
            of stars. Stored-up aromas

      the odors of incense, entrances of
            unsought light. (Yet
arrived at the waters we rubbed off

        our ointments,
            the soft
         insides of our shells

         When above, the wet flesh, the
            white flash whose One Thigh,
  the wet sun,

        turned its milk in
        our throats

Her boat of sun's burnt
odors of wood.

Bent rays of Ananse's
webbed embrace.

Moored water's (root
of Nu's) ashcolored
clouds.

Her net of
dust a veil
our dance undoes.

ii.

No boat of sun's
burnt odors of wood
bend rays of Ananse's webbed embrace.

Moored waters, root of Nu's ashcolored
clouds,
whatever newly-risen,
long-awaited sun inside
our heads,

the god's knee pushed up our crotch
whose thigh
shakes the heavens' heart.

Poem for Don Cherry

"mu" first part

The day before the
        year begins woke to a
glimpse of her
            scratchy legs

Lotusheaded, squatted
        by the side of the bed

Sat upside a Hill to
            wait for rain or
watch the sun set,

                    see
            how far the way we'd
                                come
        went back

"mu" second part

The mouth she wore
who although she wore jeans I
    could see she grew hair
        on her legs,
                    her bald feet

And at the Stream,
who in her cupped hands held it,
                            thirst,
        or some worship,
                    whichever

All the mud, alive
  with eggs, with likenesses

                              Noises
came out of it

            Calls

      teo-teo-can

                  The coarse
cloth of Moorish cante

                  The fluted
      bone of our lady's
            blown upon thigh

                        The
      enormous bell of a
            trumpet's inturned
      eye, an endangered
                        isle, some

  insistent Mu,
                  become the
            root of whatever

                        song

Outer Egypt

—"mu" third part—

Spreading her night's
garment of stars' knotted
  light, whose ragged
    edges which are lips
impress a kiss upon
              the world

(Dulled hammers, worked
as in a road of wet
    cement, where in
  the heat smells carry
             like sound

But at the brim of her
    cupped hands cures
             come
  out of trees recall Osiris
    back to life between
            her lips

(Bad clouds, out across the hills
             to the west,
  announce the wet
flash of Huracan's

        thigh

New and Old Gospel

                The pillows
         wet our faces with the
sweat of soft leaves.
         And ragmen pick the
         city like sores.

         The gummed hush of
         watered grasses fondles our
                unrest,   and as
outside the approach of
                autumn scatters all

                    our unkept secrets
         random winds unkink what
                hints your hair
lets fall.   And bits of

                        rainbow
         wet the floor and
         footsteps punish
what was silence.   As
                stars walk the

    backs of our heads our
         heads turn waking, while
                we press for what
at last will be our
                        lives to be so,

         soon.

Tarot-Teller

The
backs of her
hands, whose
        thin bones
    quiver,

    thick lips
twitch, come
    telling
            Hanged Man,

    Hermit,   Mage

And what they say
        is what you
    see, is what
                they
get you lost
            in,
                looking

    What they sow, her
hands do, say

        Let all else
                    go

    Let all else waver,

waste away to bones
        or be blown away
    blind to what we
            say we'd see

Say we see without
                looking,

          embrace but not
     touch, know the
        feel of skin we've
     yet to know or
                may never
                     caress

     Weird ragged edge
of the absolute world
          at her feet,
                     deserted
          by whose desert
     look you so love,

               the coming down
               of whose undone
                          hair

"John Coltrane Arrived with An Egyptian Lady"

— belated prayer —

no sheet of sound enshroud
the Fount of this fevered
    Brook becoming one
with God's Eye, not
   a one of these notes

   come near to the brunt
     of the inaudible
note I've been reach-
    ing towards

              To whatever
       dust-eyed giver
    of tone to whatever
talk, to whatever slack
     jaws drawn against bone

             To whatever
     hearts abulge with
unsourced light, to whatever
     sun, to whatever moist
   inward meats
             of love

     Tonight I'll bask
   beneath an arch of
             lost
  voices,   echo
    some Other place,
Nut's nether suns
            These
  notes' long fingers gathered
    come to grips of gathered

cloud, connected lip
                    to unheard of

    tongue

The Canals

*—Book of Allowing No Harm
to Be Done by Nak—*

I have eaten cakes, I have
   come forth pure as a
baby's breath, I have
      observed all rites.

               Released,
  my hips and legs are the hips
and legs of the wheeling Bear.
              The bitter
  waves announce the approach of
    an impending wind, I have
    expelled all waste.

          And
coming forth I keep to
    the side of each rush
of wind off the frozen Lake.
I lick the Sun, my lidded

    eyes unstick, light comes in
peeping up the crack between
      our burnished
           hips.

         And I
   who have not relied upon hearsay . . .
   I who have not stolen from
tombs . . .

   I who have not absorbed
  any filth or dirt of any
    kind, who have come to say I
  come forth clean, having
          come forth pure
as a baby's breath . . .

will anoint our regenerate
loins and by the light of
  Nu's darkness' chosen
                    warmths

      move seed I'll be all but
              absorbed in whose likeness,
      gnaw the roots of an exploded
                          star.

                    2

          I gathered fold
upon fold of cloth I saw
        were sun, sucked obliquities of
          unabsorbed light.
                    Reawoke
nights wanting you, my
      leg between yours, let go
  what houses we'd inhabit
                    by night.

      Now come to tell I'd come to see these
      anointed skins would in the end
              go too,

          I call the dead's
      forked-tongued insistences
                        kisses.

                              Varicose.

Bone-lipped.

          Blue.

Ohnedaruth's Day Begun

— "bright light of shipwreck" —

There I sit afloat in
the Boat of Years, a thin ellipsoid
    breath against the roof of
my mouth pressed to modulate
        pitch, reed lipped across
    time to've been wormlike,
                        earth

to become a navigable sludge.
        Sixty-eight days to my
forty-first year, this endless
    dwelling on air the key to
a courtyard filled with
    talkers, tongues in hand,
                    bush fled
    by birds whose wings burn, air
                    love's
    abrasive hush.

            These bird-gods
    anoint me with camphor, escort me
thru each a more private room, the
        chronic juices of lust flood an
                        ended earth
    whose beckoned image
                    burns on.

    Still I see no light, no
letting go of my remorse come
    shining thru, this unruly wail a not
so thickly veiled prayer you
    Anubic sisters, not a harp no
            fingers pluck played on by
                        wind.

First I'm told my false mask is
    "reformation," this horn my
                        heart's
undoing, eyes clouded with salt . . .
    the bitter coat of my rebirth
    I'll stitch of a cloth whose colors
                        run.

        In the augur's full to bursting
overload of sense mix flirts with
    meaning, says my divorced mother
    daddied me to death, my road is
                        wet,
        shows Century City against
a futuristic sun.

        So there I sit outside the
Heartbreak Straits at twenty-seven,
        sad blackened bat-winged angel, my
new day not of light but a watery
        nest. My new day roots beneath
        a basement of guts but also rises
            in the flash of my falling there.
                        Though none
    of its light comes down to me the ark of its
    rising sails.

        So again I see my-
self afloat inside this Boat of
                        Years,
    a raft of tears as Elvin's
        drumset pretends to break
    down. At the upper reach of
                        each run I

71

reach earthward, fingers blurred
while Jimmy's wrist-action
dizzies the sun. I see my ears cocked
Eastward, eyes barely open,

        beads

of sweat across my brow like rain.

        Quivering
reed between implosive teeth, Nut's tethered son,
I groan the ache of Our Lady's earth-
encumbered arch, the bell of my axe
become a wall whose bricks I
dabble on in blood as if neediness

        fed us,

the blemishless flesh of her bone-goddess
body giving birth to gloom cursing,

        "Heal

dank world. Goodbye, I'm thru,"

        all

"three" of us breathless now,
so abruptly unborn again.

        But all such
abortion compels me inward. With
bleeding fist I paw this pelvic
strath and straining ask myself to
what will Night carry me next? *ta'wil*

        to where?

pray softly, *Breath be with me*
always, bend me East of
all encumbrance, heave the
moist earth ecstatic under

        grass.

I grope thru smoke to glimpse New
York City, the Village Gate, late
     '65. I sit at the bar drinking scotch between
 sets, some kid comes up and says he'd
      like to hear "Equinox."

                              We play "Out Of
         This World" instead, the riff hits
 me like rain and like a leak in my
        throat it won't quit. No reins whoa
          this ghost I'm ridden by and again
                              I'm asking

    myself what "climb" will Nut ask of
      me next? *ta'wil* to where?
                         to what love
      turned into loss by my getting there
 as Night's reign whips on to where
                              someday
         weaned of time's ghosted light we
    begin again, our Boat as was in
                         the beginning,
        the sea itself?

                    Next I'm sipping
     wine while hearing my muse try to
        tell me which door I came in thru.
 Her thread of words a white froth at our
         feet as I forget myself,
                    limbs as
            though they were endlessly afloat,
                              a flood of
       wreckage barters wood against incestuous
                              dust.

Her splintered ships clog the sea of new
                beginnings. Beyond waking, walking
legless down where dreams unbottom our sleep,
                soaked ruins of a raft on which
                        the world outlived itself to
                bear the Heartbreak Church . . .
                                                We sit
        on pews cut from worm-infested wood.

                                        The backs
of our necks caressed by African pillows,
                the far side of her voice by
        the flutter of birds blown out to sea . . .
                While "each is both" we bask in
        an air swept clean of all distance,

                attended by bells . . .
                                Attended by
birds, in their beaks the hem of dawn's
                                        lifted
        skirts

Memphite Recension

So night sits me down be-
          fore braided Isis, I
see the moon behind a cover
                              of clouds.
          Exploding light all around us
                    nibbling our skin
                    like fish, ointments
                              oiling
          the air, all around us like
                    eyes of a religious
                              ghost looking
down above the body it leaves
                              behind . . .
                    All the times
          I'll eventually
                    recall but won't
reclaim it keeps alive,
                    the cracked
          interstices of dust . . .
                              The crushed
          coaxialities of dawn,
                    their lack of thunder's
          earthen mesh,
                              the earth
                    itself turned upon
                              an absence . . .

          Each ember of light outlives
                    any likelihood of touch, each
          previous burning's rub of
                    ash plants a rasp in
                              love's
voice . . .
          We set out across time

to what reminders of
             haunts we left the
         comforts of work loose
                         of an
almost tasteable remorse.
                     Above us black
                             revolving
         wheels turn an earthy grind, we go
             down on all fours, black
             uppity others adrift in
                         gutters
                             of light . . .

         Lidless, walking in thru one
         another's eyes, waterbabies
             both, we meet at our
                         booth inside
the Long Night Lounge whispering
         dreams and regrets, eroding
                         witnesses
                             yet

Petroglyphs inscribed in an ancient Libyan alphabet known as Tifinagh, a form of script used throughout North Africa and the Sudan. The oldest evidence of its use dates back to the 1st century, and in Mali it was used as late as the 13th. Tifinagh inscriptions have been found in various parts of the Americas, including Nova Scotia, Connecticut and elsewhere in New England. The above inscription was found beside a rockpool at Reef Bay, St. John, in the Virgin Islands. Translation: "Plunge in to cleanse and dissolve away impurity and trouble. This is water for ritual ablution before devotions."

Passing Thru

for Ivan Van Sertima

Some say the waters washing Mali's
        western edge are not the end of the world,
    that the world is like a bottlegourd.
        That a finger put at any point

                        on a bottlegourd
    and pulled across its surface
        comes at the end of its path to the
        point where it started from,

                  that so it is
with the world . . .

        And so it is with the sea
they say, plunge in, be carried west

by currents, Kouro-Siwo's black stream . . .
in search of whose pull I see them
launching their boats, my jaws
locked around a noise none of us
hears
but me.
Black pull of currents off the Gambia
coast, black sea of sweat . . .
Black flock
of birds behind a blackbearded
feathered snake,
whatever lies to the west . . .
Between two waters I rest awaiting
word of Abubakari's voyage . . .

And they've each come forth and whispered
words in my ear, these weathered
bathers,
watery dead up to their necks in
cloth.
"Snake's lift," I say,
wetting my feet, and one says
back to me, "Two slaves toast a pirate's
blood."

"Snake's glyph," to which, me
braiding my beard, the eldest
answers,
"Reef Bay virgin rockpool
worded rock."
"Or snake's lip," to which what else
can they say but that its head
goes under, tailfeathers twitch
whose twitchings quicken the wind,

what's around it shakes,

                        what else
but what inchlong ovoid nuts off a
                  palmtree
                      say?

The impatient dead go out announcing
        their immersions, dots
        and doublespiraling crescents
                    etched
      eventually as far north as
Nova Scotia . . .
           The advancing dead grope
        their way up the shoreline
                  of Amentet . . .

IV
Septet for the End of Time

"Seven," said Ogotemmêli, "is the rank of the master of Speech; $1 + 7 = 8$. The eighth rank is that of Speech itself. Speech is separate from the one who teaches it, that is, the seventh ancestor; it is the eighth ancestor. The eighth ancestor is the foundation of the speech which all the other ancestors used and which the seventh taught."

—Marcel Griaule, *Conversations with Ogotemmêli*

Some will say: "The sleepers were three: Their dog was the fourth." Others, guessing at the unknown, will say: "They were five: Their dog was the sixth." And yet others: "Seven: Their dog was the eighth."

— *The Koran*

Thy soul is provided like the star Septet.

—*Pyramid Texts of Unas*

Capricorn Rising

for Pharoah Sanders

I wake up mumbling, "I'm
      not at the music's
   mercy,"   think damned
        if I'm not, but
      keep the thought
                  to myself.

Sweet mystic beast on the
      outskirts of earth,
   unruly airs, an awkward
                        birth
        bruises the bell of its
                        horn . . .
Life after life each like it
      was endlessly yet
            to arrive yet
         already there, a
         thin bread of duress,
                        a
sea-weary drift of boatlifted
         Haitians . . .
                  The hiss of
                           the sea
         whispering words of
                        power,
      pinkish kef-pesh tools
   part the lips of the
                  dead.
         Lacking teeth but licking
            the air for some
            taste of Heaven,
                        hungered by
      its name, what of
                  it I refuse

its name, what of
                    it I refuse
forks an angel's tongue,
        what of it I refuse awakes
                the wide-eyed
                            stone

The Sleeping Rocks

for Wilson Harris

I wake up knowing it's me the rocks
    are whispering for, this
  runny watercolor dream I wake
    up from mumbling, each
    aggravated sigh like a rumble
                  underfoot.

    The chorusing rocks woo the runaway
      soul, seduce the sun, begin
        the rubbing out of innocence
                    again.
    The broken rock inside me dangling
by a thread, a thing made of glass, a thin
      gust of wind I let go of,
                breathless,
    birdheaded wraith aboard a dead
              man's boat . . .

    The chorusing rocks all repeat
  after me, say *What of it I refuse*
    forks an angel's tongue, say *What*
    of it I refuse awakes the wide-eyed
              stone,
statuesque Osiris' eyes turn earthward
    toward the thud of an apple
              as it
  hits the ground . . .
          Earth made of bonemeal
    mixed with salt. An earth baked
      by sun so bright it blackens.
    Dust in our throats a bad excuse for
a voice, though all our whispering
            shouts.

And all our whispering, altered by
   its unshown alchemy, soars,
                winged,
us having worked it so.
            I refuse this "we,"
   the chorusing rocks' echoes,
   I refuse what of earth I'll remember
                   most

Solomon's Outer Wall

I wake up sliding, rocked
asleep again, the ambiguous
      air my net of whispers,

                  banked-on
    miracle,   wasted breath . . .

Eyes wide at the exit of
      light, a deepening red
      as though they were brushed
by the wing of its return.
                  Fugitive
    sun I saw with dark-adapted

                  sight,
    so bright but unlikely, lonely
      glint of so seductive
a spark . . .

      Betrayed my own most
   inward sense of how things
              were
   that I awoke to no better,
              world
   on the run if not yet on its
   knees, begged it give us our
   Day, serenaded by
              dust . . .

I watched it all, neither "I"
   nor "other," in as well as
out, husk but heart's feathered
              itch . . .
    Stared out with wide Ethiopian
    eyes, anonymous angel,

painted face inside an
                              eight-pointed
star . . .

          I watched it go, run away
like love overshooting its mark,
                              whatever
          numbed embrace,   deep
               indigenous cut of one
          remembered kiss,   parted
                              lips
at whose meeting our repair put off
                              its end . . .

     I watched it fade, not knowing if
          I'd ever see it again, not knowing
     when if I would . . .   Crossed

          I's form an X whose arms go
     up in flames as I awake inside
               a deep, ever thickening
                              pit

Ghost of A Chance

I wake up snapped at by a star
     at the foot of a ladder,   think
I'm on my way to Heaven, fall
back tasting your tongue . . .
    Robed in water, taken back where
one evening we met, whose hearts had no
     mercy, you whisper, "Already it's

               all so far

out of reach . . . "

          Hounded by light, we
hear the heavens growl, bright snarling
beast aimed at by Ishtar's arrows, weeping

              star.
Isis to the heart's Osiris, pinkish rock . . .

              As though
a stone's eye anointed us in tears . . .

          Broken
heart, broken promise of Heaven.   Broken head

             of a ghost
    whose bitter wine we sip.

          The press of your
mouth recites a wordless vow, wet reminder
    the sea inside me rises to meet as
I fall back breathless,   boatless

          journey
to the end of the earth I wake up ambushed by.

          But not
   the first to fall,   not the first to raise Hell
    as we climb toward Heaven, call it love at
first sight,   moans caught in our throats a

          captive

angel's cry,
　　　　　　　not the first to not stop.

　　　　　　　　　　　　　　　　A crowded
upstairs flat, a quiet would-be Miles at work on
　　"Stella By Starlight," risky stair to the
　　sky . . .

　　　　　　　Seven reeds of a pipe the seven rungs
on a ladder,　　risky stares across the room, broken
　　　　shape-shifting star.　　Broken music-footed
ghost whose low tolling of chords would make
　　　　　　　　　　　　　　　　　　the still
　　waters run, would stir the wines in their
　cellars,　　pipe a thread of complaint so complete
　　the stars begin to scatter,　　panicky
　　　　　　　　　　　　　　　　music
I'd cut
　　　if I could

Winged Abyss

for Olivier Messiaen

I wake up dreaming I'm forty years in
        back of the times,   hear talk of a
    Bright Star converging on Egypt.
                                This on day

        two of this my thirty-fifth year,
    forty years out in front that I
        even hear of it at all . . .

                            Such abrupt
fallings away of the ground, such obstructions
        like a cello with one string gone.
                            An avalanche of
    light. An old out-of-tune upright, some of
        whose keys keep getting stuck . . .
    A creaking door makes me dream of colors,
            caught up in whose warp a knotted
                                        stick

        leaned on by the sun . . .

    A war camp quartet for the end of time
        heard with ears whose time has yet to
                                    begin . . .
    An unlikely music I hear makes a world
                                    break

beyond its reach . . .

                    So I wake up handed a book
        by an angel whose head has a rainbow
                                    behind it.
            I wake up holding a book announcing the
                end of time.
                            A lullaby of wings, under-
        neath whose auspices, obedient, asleep

with only one eye shut, not the
end of
the world but a bird at whose feet I hear
time
dissolve . . .

A free-beating fist, each tip of wing turned
inward. Battered gate of a City said to be
of the Heart.
Held me up as if to cleanse me
with fire, neither more nor less alive
than when
I wasn't there . . .

I hear talk.
Out of touch
with the times, I wake up asking what
bird
would make so awkward a
sound

You will live more than millions of years, an era of millions,
But in the end I will destroy everything that I have created,
The earth will become again part of the Primeval Ocean ...

— Atum to Osiris, *The Book of the Dead*

The Phantom Light of All our Day

for Jess

I wake up standing before a scene I stood
before as a child. What bits of
it I see no more than seem they were
ever there, though they'd
someday blur the broken paste-up
world
I saw
would blow itself apart ...

My back to the wall whose beginning
the day of my release brought forward, so
unlikely a start, I stand watching the
brook I stood before as a boy, no sweeter
tooth but for boundaries, bite
off more
than I can chew ...

Bittersweet kiss
of this my tightlipped muse, puckered
skin of the earth as though
its orbit
shrunk.
Shrill hiss of the sun so
much a doomsday prophet gasping voiceless,
asking,

When will all the killing
                    stop?

As though the truth were not so visibly
                    Never.
    As though the light were not all but
    drowned in the Well to the uncharted
    East I sought . . .
                    Let its blue be
my heavenly witness, I resolve before
                    the brook
        I stood before as a child . . .

            Up at dawn every day these
    days, I'm learning to look into
        the lidlessness the North Wind

                        wakes . . .
        learning to gaze into the sky
        my invented eyes unveil under
    acid rain, chemical sunsets, blush

                        of a
shotgun bride.

        The grass blowing east at the
    merest mention of wind where
            there is no wind, no place for
        a horse in this the riderless

                        world.
    I'm learning to paint. I repeat
these words as an irritable mystic, my
        would-be hum, neither life
        nor limb not on the edge of
            dislocation, some such

                        dance

I dare . . .

But still I stand before
the brook I stood before as a boy.
Thicknesses of paint, as if
                              the eye
looked into its looking, let the skull
              show thru, show the Kings of
Xibalba play with poison gas and me
              among them, 1940s' chemical
                              warfare corps . . .

I'm learning to see, says my enamored mage, what's
      going on. I hear the rumbling in the music I
paint.

      Luminous breezes locked in the nucleus'
      inmost reaches echo Atum's vow. These
              radiant winds obey the abandon our
      learning sought.

I stand watching the brook I stood before
      as a boy, the painted echo of
      a snapshot my father took. The oils
                              thicken
my sleep,
      the unuprootable oath I wake up to,
                              the earth
a part of Ocean
              again

Falso Brilhante

for Elis Regina

I wake up chasing my breath, my
dead lungs undone by alcohol and cocaine,
a rope of dust at my throat . . .
Raw thread of a dirge woven into the
wind, all night I wonder
what
but unruliness ranges the heart . . .

A blunt featherless
bird hovering close to my chest as
I wake up, what but ennui that I'd even
wonder, what but a whim, the clouded rum
I drink   drains me of light
I dream I hang from, dangling,

draped
as in rags, white fractured sky from which
I fall . . .
White sky made blue by the blackness
beyond it, withered light, wind says *Better*

not
to have been born.
Breath caught in
a cloud, I cross myself, *So be it,*
my self-embrace
a rickety crib I serenade
myself
inside . . .
And I'm singing all the songs that made me a
star, my arms like wings as though
they were not quite my own anymore . . .

Leaned
on by a ghost, I launch a prayer to Iansã, Ogum
at my back, my torn voice haloed

by an orbiting chorus as it bleeds,
hand on my heart as if I were taking an

oath,

a faint, fading
spark, the seeds of this parting planted
who knows how far back . . .

A see-thru lid on the coffin I rest in.
See-thru exit, see-thru sign of the times . . .
Weepers fill the streets of São Paulo,
I wake up gasping,   chasing my breath,

another
snuffed-out star.   Prophetic wingtip skimming
the water . . .
A crystalline cut color makes

in time . . .
In every crack the same suffocating sweat,

this

world with its arrows . . .
Its rosary of worms, its
neon angels, its megatons . . .

One eye with
God, the other eye with Satan, I watch the
empty-eyed, pipe-smoking saints . . .

The keepers of bread do with the world as they

will,

whose cards collapse . . .
The way the
wind has of having its way
with a falling

leaf

Dogon Eclipse

I wake up waved at, said goodbye
    to, wondering what now,
    what "I" keeps me up.
                                I
    wake up eyeless, blinded, eyed,
watched over by armies,   cautious,
                                        caught.

    Waved at by lines of disappearing
        kin, sleeves woven by Night
        of light lured from the sun . . .
            So like a refugee's tilted boat,
    white
                light of shipwreck. Dog's
                    teeth. Snarling star . . .

I see no boats but hear the waters break,
        their breaking weights us
        with the chill of a remembered
                                        flood.

Digitaria seed, orbited snake's tooth, Eye
        Star.   Dog Star.   Lidless.
                                    Bright.

    A debt of bullets taken years before
        as I fall back blinded . . . Up-
        start sun I slip thru careful not to
        cross my legs and as my
                                gun misfires
        feel I've boarded one of Marcus'
erratic ships, aborted Black Star Line,
                                    prophetic
                        ark of unrest . . .

                    ark of unrest . . .
          Withered lid of an eroded "I,"
          Ogotemmêli overlooks the lit city
outside,
                    the rough-throated weavers
                    of secrets whispering endlessly
                                        that
                    "nothing ever was anyway . . . "
                    Hears the sound of some unheard-of
                                                  horn
so far away not even wings or weathered legs
                would get us there . . .
                                   Hears the drum the
     djinns tie to the sky, Tabele,
               beat, its rhythms waste
               us, weightless dream and
                                   so ended
          search . . .

               All as though one's
          feet would find their way without
                                   escort.
               All as if by then I'd
                                   been thru
Hell
          and back

Poetry from Illinois

History Is Your Own Heartbeat
Michael S. Harper (1971)

The Foreclosure
Richard Emil Braun (1972)

The Scrawny Sonnets and
Other Narratives
Robert Bagg (1973)

The Creation Frame
Phyllis Thompson (1973)

To All Appearances: Poems New
and Selected
Josephine Miles (1974)

Nightmare Begins Responsibility
Michael S. Harper (1975)

The Black Hawk Songs
Michael Borich (1975)

The Wichita Poems
Michael Van Walleghen (1975)

Cumberland Station
Dave Smith (1977)

Tracking
Virginia R. Terris (1977)

Poems of the Two Worlds
Frederick Morgan (1977)

Images of Kin: New and
Selected Poems
Michael S. Harper (1977)

On Earth as It Is
Dan Masterson (1978)

Riversongs
Michael Anania (1978)

Goshawk, Antelope
Dave Smith (1979)

Death Mother and Other Poems
Frederick Morgan (1979)

Local Men
James Whitehead (1979)

Coming to Terms
Josephine Miles (1979)

Searching the Drowned Man
Sydney Lea (1980)

With Akhmatova at the Black Gates
Stephen Berg (1981)

More Trouble with the Obvious
Michael Van Walleghen (1981)

Dream Flights
Dave Smith (1981)

The American Book of the Dead
Jim Barnes (1982)

Northbook
Frederick Morgan (1982)

The Floating Candles
Sydney Lea (1982)

Collected Poems, 1930–83
Josephine Miles (1983)

The River Painter
Emily Grosholz (1984)

The Passion of the
Right-Angled Man
T. R. Hummer (1984)

Healing Song for the Inner Ear
Michael S. Harper (1984)

Poems from the Sangamon
John Knoepfle (1985)

Eroding Witness
Nathaniel Mackey (1985)
National Poetry Series